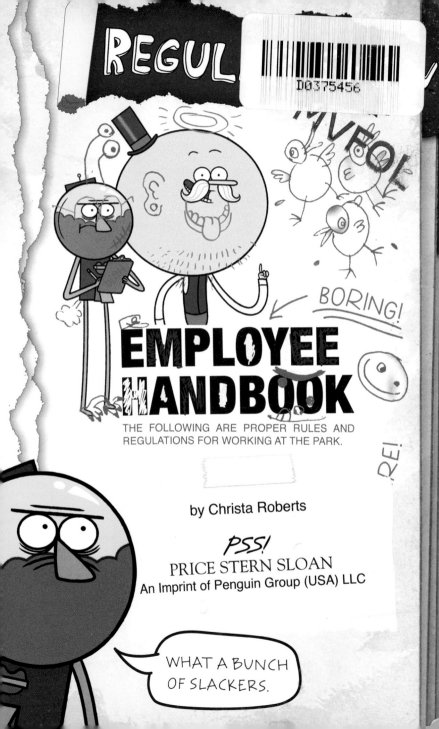

REGUL

D0375456

BORING!

# EMPLOYEE HANDBOOK

THE FOLLOWING ARE PROPER RULES AND
REGULATIONS FOR WORKING AT THE PARK.

by Christa Roberts

*PSS!*
PRICE STERN SLOAN
An Imprint of Penguin Group (USA) LLC

WHAT A BUNCH
OF SLACKERS.

PRICE STERN SLOAN
Published by the Penguin Group
Penguin Group (USA) LLC, 375 Hudson Street, New York, New York 10014, USA

USA I Canada I UK I Ireland I Australia I New Zealand I India I South Africa I China

penguin.com
A Penguin Random House Company

Photo credits: page 5, 7, 8, 25, 26, 31, 37, 43, 44, 59, 60, 61, 62: (burned paper) © iStock/Thinkstock; page 9, 19, 35, 39, 43, 49, 74: (collage paper smudge) © iStock/Thinkstock; page 10: (color sticky notes) © Wavebreak Media/Thinkstock; page 15, 16, 34, 36, 37, 38, 41, 42, 43, 64, 65, 71, 76, 77: (retro yellow paper) © Hemera/Thinkstock; page 18, 19, 22, 23, 27, 31, 33, 39, 41, 42, 44, 47, 58, 69, 70, 72, 79, 80: (animal tracks) © iStock/Thinkstock; page 22, 23, 27, 44, 80: (bird poop) © iStock/Thinkstock; page 40, 41, 42: (notepaper) © iStock/Thinkstock; page 43: (math paper) © iStock/Thinkstock; page 49, 50, 51, 53: (fingerprint & footprint) © Hemera/Thinkstock.

Published in 2013 by Price Stern Sloan, a division of Penguin Young Readers Group, 345 Hudson Street, New York, New York 10014. PSS! is a registered trademark of Penguin Group (USA) LLC. Printed in the U.S.A.

ISBN 978-0-8431-7743-5          10 9 8 7 6 5 4 3 2 1

# REGULAR SHOW

## Employee Handbook

**Table of Contents**

WHOA, DUDE, THERE'S A TON OF RULES HERE.

Welcome to the Park! Here in the official *Employee Handbook,* you'll find the answers to all your questions about your job. I am pleased to welcome you to a community of happy, healthy, and thriving employees. Working together, we can achieve anything we set our minds to! Take pride in yourselves, your job, and your park. Everything you need to know about working in the Park is here, in this handy, easy-to-follow reference book.

Yours truly,

Benson,
Park Manager

*The management reserves the right at any time and for any reason to change park policies and guidelines, with no further notice whatsoever.

DUDE, CHeCK it OUt. LOOKS LiKe SOMEONE'S going ON a LittLe POWeR tRiP, CReatiNg a HaNDbOOK FOR tHe emPLOYees.

I'm sick and tired of all the slacking off going on around here. I have better things to do than to constantly check up on everyone to make sure they're doing the jobs they're getting paid to do. I could be listening to music. Playing cricket. Catching up on my reading. I am D-O-N-E done with answering the same questions over and over and over again. So, I've put together an *Employee Handbook*. Everyone who works in the Park needs to read it, use it, and follow ALL the rules laid out in it. And to make sure everyone has read it, every employee (that's YOU) must sign this acknowledgment:

I, _connor_ , understand, completely respect, and accept all the rules outlined in this, the *Employee Handbook*.

6

RIGHT, DUDE, BUT I THINK WE'RE GOING TO HAVE TO READ IT. WE WANT TO KEEP OUR JOBS AT THE PARK, DON'T WE, RIGBY?

PFFFFT! YEAH. I GUESS.

SO LET'S JUST READ THROUGH THE STUPID THING AND SIGN OFF ON IT. JUST BECAUSE WE SIGN IT DOESN'T MEAN WE HAVE TO DO WHAT IT SAYS.

HEH, HEH, YOU'RE RIGHT, BRO. SINCE WHEN DID SIGNING ON THE DOTTED LINE MEAN YOU WERE PROMISING YOUR LIFE AWAY?

I THINK A HANDBOOK FOR EMPLOYEES IS AN ABSOLUTELY WONDERFUL IDEA. DO I GET MY OWN COPY?

Okay, technically speaking, Pops is my boss, but in reality, it's his father, Mr. Maellard, who calls the shots around this place. **He's** my real boss. And I sure hope that he's impressed with this. Not that I would open up to any of the idiots that work here, but I'm always riding their butts because **my** boss is always on **my** back. He calls me names and blames **me** for every screwup.

YOU GUYS KNOW I'M NOT PLAYING HERE. I'VE FIRED PEOPLE BEFORE, AND I'LL DO IT AGAIN IF I HAVE TO.

AND THEN YOU'LL REHIRE US. BECAUSE YOU'RE ALL TALK, BENSON.

# Working in the Park

**Mission statement: Working in the Park is both a privilege and an honor. Each employee should treat the Park as if it were his or her own home. Respect your park and your park manager, and they will respect you back.**

PFFFT! SO NOW WE HAVE A MISSION STATEMENT.

HA-HA, MORE LIKE PERMISSION-TO-DO-WHATEVER-WE-FEEL-LIKE STATEMENT.

BECAUSE IN MY HOUSE, I ALWAYS CARVE OUT A LITTLE SPACE FOR WHAT I LIKE TO CALL RIGBY TIME. BREAK OUT A BIG BOWL OF WHAT I LIKE TO CALL CHIPS, PARK MYSELF ON WHAT I LIKE TO CALL **THE COUCH**, AND LET WHAT I LIKE TO CALL **THE VIDEO GAMING** BEGIN. ANYONE UP FOR A LITTLE **ZOMBIE'S RETURN 4**?

YES AND YES.

HMM! HMM! HMM!!!

YOU KNOW WHAT ELSE IS BETTER THAN WORKING? BLASTING THE TUNES.

AND beat-boxin' and channel surfin'. Doin' it OLD SCHOOL.

AND ORDERING PIZZA AND WINGS EVERY HOUR ON THE HOUR STARTING AT MIDNIGHT. "HELLO, PIZZA PLACE? IT'S ME, MORDECAI. I NEED ANOTHER PEPPERONI PIZZA AND A DOUBLE ORDER OF GOLD-PLATED CHICKEN WINGS. YOU KNOW THE ADDRESS."

DUDE, THAT'S RAD. AND YOU KNOW WHAT ELSE IS RAD? VIDEO-GAME POWER PARTY!!!!

OHHHHH!

ALL PLAY AND NO WORK MAKES RIGBY REALLY HAPPY.

HA-HA-HA-HA-HA!

14

# Mutual Respect

I, Rigby, ripped out Benson's stupid pages about respect and taped in this. Because **THIS** is important. People need to know what the worst jobs are so they can **NOT** do them.

## WORST JOBS IN THE PARK

THESE JOBS **STINK!**

- Cleaning the fountain.
  Dude, this job is **LAME.** I hate this job!

- Cleaning the men's room toilets.
  Avoid at all costs.

- Making Benson's breakfast

- Picking up trash ← GUM STUCK UNDER THE PARK BENCHES? **THE WORST.**

- Snack bar → THIS IS THE **WORST** OF THE **WORST.** I HATE BEING STUCK IN THE SNACK BAR.

  DUDE, YOU'VE GOT IT ALL WRONG. I LOVE BEING IN THE SNACK BAR. SELL ONE SNACK, EAT TWO MORE. THAT'S HOW THE GOOD TIMES ROLL IN SNACK LAND.

- Disinfecting the kiddie pool

- Scooping poop    PICK UP AFTER YOUR DOG, PEOPLE. **IT'S NOT THAT HARD.**

- CHASING DOWN LITTERBUGS

- GIVING PEOPLE DIRECTIONS

POINTING PEOPLE IN THE WRONG DIRECTION IS PRETTY HILARIOUS! "OH, YOU'RE LOOKING FOR THE PADDLEBOATS. THEY'RE THAT WAY . . . IN THE PARKING LOT!" HEH, HEH, HEH.

THAT'S NOT VERY NICE, RIGBY.

- WEEDING

- TRIMMING SHRUBBERY

- MULCHING

- SPRAYING HORNETS WITH INSECT REPELLENT

GETTING STUNG BY A STUPID BEE IS SO NOT COOL.

- MOWING THE GRASS

- FERTILIZING

r backwa

Totally and utterly gra

16

# Timekeeping

When it comes to working in the Park, nothing matters more than punctuality, reliability, and trustworthiness.

THE ONLY time I CARE about is Some quality bRo time. Right, MORDECAI?

YOU GOT IT, RIGBY.

TO CLEAR UP ANY CONFUSION ON TIME, LET ME SPELL IT OUT FOR YOU:

A FULL-TIME EMPLOYEE WORKS FORTY HOURS.

A PART-TIME EMPLOYEE WORKS TWENTY HOURS OR LESS.

AND THEN THERE'S MORDECAI AND RIGBY.

I THOUGHT HE Was GOING TO SPELL IT OUT.

If you need to take a day off, you must report it to your supervisor. Missing a shift that you are scheduled to work is a bad idea. Let's explore further. We'll use fictional examples.

## GOOD EMPLOYEE BEHAVIOR

"I need next Monday off. I have a dental check-up," Pips says. "Skops has offered to cover for me."

"Thank you, Pips. I will mark that change on the calendar. I appreciate you being so responsible," Babson says.

## BAD EMPLOYEE BEHAVIOR

"The fountain is a mess! Who was supposed to clean it?" Babson asks.

"Rugby," Metal Man says. "He never showed up at work today. I saw him and Medici doing wheelies in the golf cart."

"Sigh," says Babson. "That is a real problem. Now we all must look at a dirty fountain. If only Rugby would have done the right thing and reported to work when he was scheduled to, that problem would have been avoided."

THIS STINKS, MAN. WHY AM I BEING USED AS THE BAD EXAMPLE?
AND WHAT'S UP WITH THAT *MEDICI* BALONEY? DUDE, IF YOU'RE GONNA USE FAKE NAMES, YOU'VE GOTTA DO BETTER THAN THAT.
OH, DON'T GET UPSET, BOYS. IT'S NOT YOU TWO IN THE STORY. DIDN'T YOU LISTEN? IT'S RUGBY AND MEDICI. IT'S JUST A MADE-UP STORY. IT'S NOT REAL. RIGHT, BABSON?

# Paid Holidays

**Easter**

**Thanksgiving**

**Christmas**

THAT'S IT? THREE DAYS? THAT'S THE LAMEST THING I'VE EVER HEARD. DON'T EXPECT TO SEE ME ON HALLOWEEN, MAN. I'M JUST SAYIN'.

YOU KNOW WHO ELSE YOU'LL NEVER SEE ON HALLOWEEN? MY MOM!

THERE ARE MANY WONDERFUL BENEFITS TO WORKING HERE AT THE PARK, AND PAID HOLIDAYS ARE JUST THE BEGINNING. NOT ONLY DO WORKERS GET TO SPEND THEIR DAYS BASKING IN THE NATURAL BEAUTY OF THE WORLD AROUND THEM, THEY ALSO HAVE A BOUNTIFUL ARRAY OF BREAK OPTIONS DURING THE WORKDAY.

Each employee can take one ten-minute break every four hours. But remember: just because you are on a break doesn't mean visitors to the Park aren't watching you. Conduct yourselves accordingly at all times.

ONE bREAK EVERY FOUR HOURS bLOWS, DUDE. IS THAT A MISPRINT? 'CAUSE I THINK YOU MEANT TO SAY ONE bREAK EVERY FOUR **MINUTES**.

YEAH, DUDE, IF YOU WORK FOR MORE THAN FOUR MINUTES AT A TIME, YOU RISK PULLIN' A HAMMY.

IF YOU get bORED, DO WHAT WE DO: take a bREAK.

A work-life balance is important to maintain. Manage your time wisely. Here at the Park, we understand that our employees have a life "outside." We've discovered that a successful employee learns to manage his time effectively. We encourage our employees to take advantage of their downtime, so that when they are at the Park, they come to work refreshed, invigorated, and ready to work!

"Time management"? Benson should learn how to manage his own time and not waste it writing fake stories about people named Rugby.

Yeah, it would have been way more accurate if he just used your real name.

Stop talking!!!

Heh, heh, heh . . .

All employees should pay special attention to this section of the handbook. (I'm talking to you, Mordecai and Rigby.) I can hear you complaining already: "We need a break, Benson. I'm not feeling well, Benson. I came in early this morning, Benson. I can't stay late, Benson. I'm too busy not working to hear you, Benson." Stuff it. I'm sick and tired of supervising a bunch of slackers. Things are going to change around here.

I'M A PRETTY PUNCTUAL GUY. SURE, I ADMIT IT—SOMETIMES RIGBY AND I MIGHT BE A LITTLE LATE. BUT THERE'S ALWAYS A REALLY GOOD REASON WHEN THAT HAPPENS.
BECAUSE GOIN' TO WORK EARLY IS FOR SUCKAAAAS!!!! UP HIGH!
DUDE, YOU KNOW THIS IS WHY BENSON WRITES ABOUT US LIKE THIS, RIGHT?
OH YEAH . . .

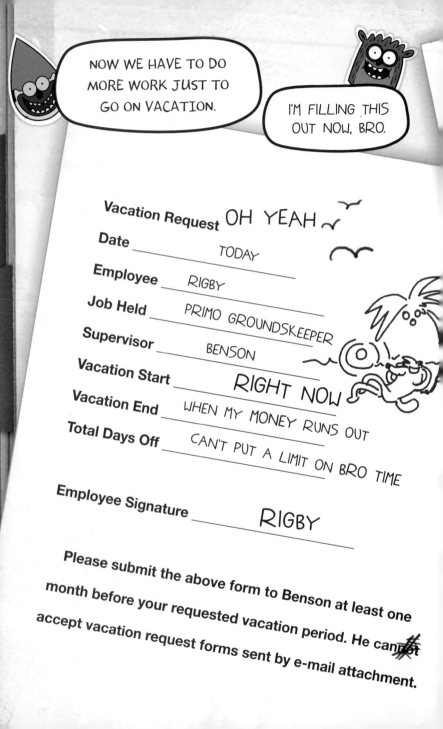

29

HEY, MORDECAI, LOOK WHAT I FOUND IN MY COPY OF THE HANDBOOK—A MEMO FROM BENSON ABOUT FIRING US. CHECK IT:

# The Firing of Mordecai and Rigby

To whom it may concern:

Mordecai and Rigby are lazy slackers. They contribute practically nothing to the Park. In fact, they've almost destroyed it on several occasions. It is my recommendation that their employment be terminated immediately.

Sincerely,

Benson, Park Manager

AWW, MAN. THAT'S NOT COOL. BUT, RIGBY, YOU KNOW IF WE GET CAUGHT WITH THIS HE'LL TOTALLY FIRE US.

IF HE'S PLANNING ON FIRING US, THEN WE'RE ALREADY FIRED, RIGHT? IT'S NOT LIKE HE CAN DOUBLE FIRE US OR SOMETHING.

LET'S MAKE SOME CHANGES ON IT AND STICK IT BACK IN HIS DESK. THAT WAY, IF HE MAILS IT TO MR. MAELLARD, IT SAYS ALL COOL THINGS AND NOT THAT OTHER STUFF. DEAL?

OKAY, YOU GOT A PEN?

WAY AHEAD OF YOU, bRO.

# The ~~Firing~~ HIRING of Mordecai and Rigby

**To whom it may concern:** beacons of awesomeness in a DaRK, DREaRY WORLD

**Mordecai and Rigby are** ~~lazy slackers.~~

**They contribute** EVERYTHING TO THE PARK THAT MAKES IT WORTH GOING TO. THEY ARE THE PARK.

~~**Park. In fact, they've almost destroyed it on**~~ MY ability to even HIRE a NEW employee on

**several occasions.** ~~It is my recommendation~~

—BECAUSE NO ONE CAN COMPARE TO THE EXAMPLE THESE TWO HARD WORKERS HAVE SET. THEY'VE SET THE BAR VERY HIGH. IN FACT, I THINK THEY'RE OVERQUALIFIED, AND SHOULD PROBABLY JUST BE THE **PRESIDENTS** OF THE UNITED STATES.

**that their employment be** ~~te~~ PERMANENT, AND tHat tHeY ~~.~~ ReCeIVe bIg Fat RaIses, PRESIDENT STYLE, i.e., get PaID In gIant OVERSIZE NOVELtY CHECKS, IMMEDIatELY.

**Sincerely,**

Benson, Park Manager

# A Note from Benson, aka, the Boss

You might be thinking that I'm a little hot-tempered, sarcastic, maybe even mean. Well, you're right. You would be, too, if you had morons like Mordecai and Rigby working for you. They are constantly—and I mean constantly—slacking off. I can't trust them. They require around-the-clock supervision. I should have fired them a long time ago. Can you say *does not meet expectations*? But you can't say that I'm too hot-tempered, sarcastic, or mean. I haven't fired them yet, have I?

MORONS? MORONS? I'LL TELL YOU WHO'S A MORON. YOU ARE, BENSON, FOR WRITING THESE LIES. AND I'M GONNA DRAW ALL OVER YOUR LITTLE NOTEY-NOTE. BAM!
MAYBE WE SHOULDN'T DO THIS. THIS IS THE KIND OF THING THAT COULD GET US FIRED.
THAT'S EXACTLY WHY WE SHOULD DO IT—IF WE'RE GOING TO GET FIRED EVENTUALLY, WHY PROLONG THE INEVITABLE?

I can be Mr. Nice Guy. I like rewarding people who work. I give them time off. I even give them raises.

YEAH, LIKE A DOLLAR A YEAR.

HE GAVE ME a COUPON FOR a FREE SINGLE-SCOOP ICE-CREaM CONE aT DaIREE DELITE. I WENT OUT THaT NIGHT TO USE IT.

WITH WHO?

MY MOM! BUT IT WaS ExPIRED.

Treating people fairly is important to me. Do you think I like freaking out? Do you think I like getting so mad that I turn into a ball of energy and almost destroy the Park?

YEAH, MAN, I DO. YOU'RE ALWAYS FLIPPING OUT AND LOSING YOUR COOL OVER STUFF. DON'T SWEAT THE SMALL STUFF, BRO. IT'S SMALL. DON'T SWEAT ON IT.

> *SAGE ADVICE, MORDECAI.*
> *SAGE ADVICE!*

Unfortunately some people just know how to push my buttons, like Mordecai and Rigby. I have a short fuse with those two. I don't hate them—I just want them to listen to me when I yell at them. Is that too much to ask?

> UH, YEAH.

At least Mordecai shows some maturity now and then. It's Rigby who's the troublemaker. He brings them both down.

> SAY WHAT?

They don't get it: If they screw up it looks bad for me, the boss, and then I could lose my job. I don't want to lose my job. I'm tired of having to always tell people what to do. I don't want to be the bad guy. So hopefully this book will put an end to their bad behavior.

ARE WE GOING TO SIT BY AND JUST TAKE THAT LOAD FROM HIM?

UH, YEAH. WE ARE. HE'S OUR BOSS.

OH, RIGHT.

# Employee Opinion Survey

## The Park Needs YOU!

**The management wants to hear YOUR opinion. What's important to you, the employees? How could we make things better?**

40

YEAH. AND DON'T KEEP US IN THE DARK ABOUT STUFF, MAN. IF SOMETHING'S GOING DOWN, TELL US ABOUT IT. WE DON'T WANT TO BE THE LAST TO KNOW.

YEAH, IF YOU'RE GONNA FIRE US, GIVE US SOME ADVANCE WARNING.

43

# MONEY, MONEY, MONEY

Everyone who works at the Park is to be paid fairly and squarely, in a timely fashion. Pay day is semimonthly, on the fifteenth and the last day of the month. Direct deposit is available, and the Park will also continue to pay by check and in some cases, sandwich baggies containing coins. The park management also has an excellent benefits program that includes:

- Two weeks paid vacation

- Five sick days

- Medical, dental, and vision insurance

- 401(k) savings plan

- Bowling team

- Discount dry-cleaning coupon at We Clean Your Stuff! (10 percent off)

> WOULD IT BE POSSIBLE TO TAKE ONE HOUR OF VACATION EVERY DAY?

Details for all these programs are available in the manager's office.

YOU KNOW WHO ELSE IS AVAILABLE IN THE MANAGER'S OFFICE? MY MOM!
THIS GUT'S FOR YOU
BASICALLY WE'RE HERE FOR TWO REASONS: MONEY AND FREE RENT.
YOU KNOW IT!
FIVE WHOLE DAYS OF BEING SICK? THAT SOUNDS SIMPLY AWFUL!
HEY, POPS. THAT DOESN'T MEAN YOU HAVE TO BE SICK FOR FIVE DAYS—JUST THAT IF YOU ARE, YOU'LL GET PAID FOR IT.
YEAH, POPS. LIKE WHEN YOU TAKE A MENTAL-HEALTH DAY TO PLAY VIDEO GAMES AND STILL GET PAID FOR IT. WHICH ESSENTIALLY MEANS WE'RE PROFESSIONAL GAMERS!

**Employees who excel at their jobs have the chance to:**

- **Get raises**

- **Get an extra day off**

- **Be the Park's "Employee of the Month." This very special honor comes with an engraved Employee of the Month plaque, suitable for hanging, and preferred parking for the month of the employee's choice.**

## EXPECTATIONS

We maintain very high standards for everyone who works in the Park. It is crucial that every employee who steps onto the park grounds conducts himself with dignity.

> WHAT HAPPENS IF I'M IN THE MIDDLE OF JUMPING? BETCHA DIDN'T THINK OF THAT, NOW, DID YA? THE AIR DOESN'T COUNT AS THE PARK, BENSON!

Remember, you are a role model to not only visitors to the Park, but to each other. Disrespect to visitors or other employees will not be tolerated. The Park should be considered a "harassment-free" zone.

> DUDE, DID YOU HEAR THAT? WE'RE ROLE MODELS.

> YEAH, PEOPLE WANT TO BE JUST LIKE US. PROBABLY BECAUSE WE'RE 100 PERCENT AWESOME.

**If in doubt, remember these Do's and Don'ts:**

## Do:

**Show up on time. If your shift begins at 9:00 a.m., don't walk in at 9:01 a.m. And leaving early is frowned upon and requires permission from your ~~supervisor~~.**

> WHAT IF MY SHIFT BEGINS AT 10:00 AND I WALK IN AT 9:01? DO I GET EXTRA CREDIT?

> HA-HA, YEAH, AND WHY WOULD I WANT TO LEAVE EARLY? IT'S NOT LIKE I'D HAVE ANYTHING IMPORTANT TO DO— LIKE LIVE MY LIFE.

**Cover your tattoos while working in public areas.**

*I ONCE ENTERTAINED THE IDEA OF GETTING A TATTOO ON MY—*

WHOA! WHOA, POPS! WE DON'T NEED TO HEAR THIS.

YEAH, THERE'S NO REASON FOR US TO BE MENTALLY SCARRED. KEEP IT TO YOURSELF, POPS.

**Remember: A smile is your best accessory.**

*SMILE AND THE WORLD SMILES WITH YOU!*

YOU KNOW WHO HAS A GREAT SMILE? MY MOM!

## Don't:

**Be offensive.**

**This will get you fired.**

THIS bOOK OFFENDS Me. DOES tHAt MeAN YOU'Re gONNA FIRe it?

**Harass fellow coworkers, supervisors, or subordinates.**

**This will get you fired.**

DOES SeeING BENSON'S FACe COUNt AS HARASSMENt? BOO-YEAH.

DUDE, COOL IT! THAT'S KINDA HARASSMENT.

OH . . . JUSt KIDDING, BENSON!

**Wear clothing with crude messages.**

**This will get you fired.**

YEAH, YOU BETTER NOT WEAR THE *WORK IS FOR TURDS* SHIRT YOU GOT CUSTOM-MADE AT THE MALL LAST WEEK, RIGBY.

WHY NOt? I WAS ONLY gONNA WeAR it WHEN WE WEREN'T WORKING, AND WHEN SOMEONE—COUGH, BENSON, COUGH!—WAS WORKING. It WOULDA BEEN HILARIOUS.

**Be a lazy slacker.**

**This will get you fired.**

I FEEL LIKE HE'S TALKING ABOUT US WITHOUT TALKING ABOUT US.

DUDE, HE'S TOTALLY TALKING ABOUT US.

WELL, WHY?? WE'RE NOT SLACKERS—WE JUST TAKE A LOT OF BREAKS, WHICH ARE TOTALLY OWED TO US. BENSON SAID SO HIMSELF EARLIER IN THIS DUMB BOOK!

**If you have a complaint, there is an official form you will need to fill out. Complaint forms are available in the park manager's office.**

I hate to even mention complaint forms—that's all slackers like the jerks who work here need to hear about. But the bigwigs that own this park said we have to put this in the handbook or else we can get into all sorts of legal trouble.

That's why I put this thing together in the first place. What if one of the park employees got mad and decided to sue? I don't think any of them would have a case, but still. I needed something that would protect the park and cover yours truly.

HEY, KNOW WHAT? THOSE *DON'TS DO* STINK!

OOH, THAT SOUNDS LIKE A COMPLAINT, RIGBY! DON'T FORGET TO FILE AN OFFICIAL COMPLAINT FORM. I HAVE AN OFFICIAL PARK PEN IF YOU NEED ONE.

THANKS, POPS, BUT I THINK RIGBY WAS JUST EXPRESSING HIMSELF. HE DOESN'T WANT TO FILE AN OFFICIAL COMPLAINT. RIGHT, RIGBY?

*Riiiight.* OR MAYBE I SHOULD EXPRESS MYSELF BY FILING A COMPLAINT!

I CAN EXPRESS THE FACT THAT I DON'T GET ENOUGH BREAKS. CAN I FILE A COMPLAINT?

55

# The Park Dress Code (and Other Things

**Employees Need to Know About Working in the Park)**

Here at the Park, we like to keep it casual. No stuffy suits and ties or official uniforms.

I DON'T EVEN WEAR PANTS!

MUSCLE MAN GOES TOPLESS . . . AND BRALESS.

WHY WOULD I WEAR a BRa, BRO? I'M a DUDE.

NO REASON, HEH, HEH . . .

COUNT ME IN FOR A STUFFY SUIT, PLEASE, ALONG WITH A BUTTONED-UP VEST. IT'S MY UNOFFICIAL OFFICIAL UNIFORM!

For those of you who do decide to wear clothes, keep this in mind: what you wear to work does one of two things:

1. Makes your coworkers and the park community comfortable.
2. Makes your coworkers and the park community uncomfortable.

The Park's number-one goal is for employees to be number one: comfortable. But that doesn't mean we don't have standards.

If you think something might offend a coworker, play it safe: Don't wear it. Something you wear to the beach, to a party, or to hang out at home might not be right for your job at the Park. If the park management is unhappy with your choice of clothing, you will get a warning. Multiple warnings will result in disciplinary action.

WOULDN'T THAT BE WEIRD IF HI FIVE GHOST WENT TO A BEACH PARTY AND THEN CAME TO WORK WEARING THE SAME THING AND HE GOT FIRED?

MUSCLE MAN, THERE ARE GOING TO BE EXCEPTIONS TO THE RULES.

YOU KNOW WHO ELSE IS AN EXCEPTION TO THE RULE? MY MOM!

HA-HA-HA!

I RECEIVED AN ENGRAVED RODEO BELT BUCKLE FOR MY BIRTHDAY. WOULD THAT BE OKAY TO WEAR?

SURE, POPS. WHY NOT?

61

I'M JUST NOT COMFORTABLE WEARING SHOES. NEVER HAVE BEEN.

SKIPS'S FEET HAVE TO BE FREE! HA-HA-HA!

DUDE, MORDECAI, WHY IS POPS LAUGHING? THAT'S NOT EVEN FUNNY.

I KNOW, BUT JUST LAUGH ALONG ANYWAY SO HE WON'T FEEL BAD.

HA-HA-HA! HA-HA-HA!

GOOD ONE, POPS!

**Falling asleep on the job is a big no-no. Workers need to stay awake at all times.**

I CAN'T TELL YOU HOW MANY TIMES I'VE CAUGHT MORDECAI AND RIGBY ASLEEP ON THE JOB. WHAT KIND OF EMPLOYEE DOES THAT? LAZY BUMS LIKE THOSE TWO.

63

BLAH BLAH BLAH

OKAY, THIS IS THE STUPIDEST THING EVER, AND I AM CROSSING OUT EVERY STUPID WORD. BENSON WANTED TO WRITE ABOUT HOW HE WANTS TO PROMOTE PEOPLE WHO DO THEIR JOBS WELL AND STUFF.

WHAT A BUNCH OF GARBAGE. BENSON'S NOT INTERESTED IN JOB PERFORMANCE. HE JUST WANTS TO MAKE OUR LIVES AS MISERABLE AS HIS IS.

DUDE, YOU SAID IT. LAST YEAR HE GAVE ME A REVIEW, RIGHT? EXCEPT HE WAITED UNTIL MY REVIEW TO TELL ME WHAT MY GOALS WERE SUPPOSED TO BE FOR THE PAST YEAR.

AND AFTER THAT, HE TOLD ME I WASN'T EVEN GETTING A COST-OF-LIVING RAISE. HE SAID HE KNEW I WORKED AT THE PARK BECAUSE I LOVED IT—THAT HE KNEW I WASN'T HERE FOR THE MONEY.

TYPICAL FOR SLACKERS: THEY DON'T WANT TO KNOW HOW TO IMPROVE. IT'S A VERY SIMPLE CONCEPT: GOOD WORK CAN GET YOU PROMOTED. BAD WORK CAN GET YOU DEMOTED.
I REMEMBER THAT YOU GOT DEMOTED ONCE, BENSON. REMEMBER?
IF YOU KNOW WHAT'S GOOD FOR YOU, YOU'LL SHUT YOUR TRAP ABOUT THAT ONE. OR YOU'RE FIRED!

67

## Appreciation Day

This is a special day here at the Park. We love catching our employees doing good things! Praise for work well done is the highlight of Appreciation Day. Everyone looks forward to it. Photos of last year's Appreciation Day are on display in the manager's office.

REMEMBER THAT ONE APPRECIATION DAY WHERE EVERYONE BUT RIGBY AND I GOT PLAQUES?

THOSE BAD MEMORIES HAUNT ME TO THIS DAY.

BENSON GAVE POPS A PLAQUE FOR HELPING A BABY BIRD BACK INTO HIS NEST. AND HE GAVE SKIPS ONE FOR NOT TAKING A DAY OFF ALL YEAR. AND WE DIDN'T GET ANYTHING.

*Laaaaame.*

SO HERE ARE SOME THINGS WE'D LIKE TO BE CONSIDERED FOR THE NEXT APPRECIATION DAY.

YEAH. WE'D APPRECIATE THAT.

- APPReciate that WHEN We FALL ASLEEP ON THE JOB, We'Re eventually gonna Wake UP and PRObably FiNiSH tHe Job.

- APPRECIATE THAT JUST BECAUSE YOU CAN'T SEE SOMEONE WORKING HARD, IT DOESN'T MEAN THEY AREN'T.

- APPReciate OUR DiFFeReNces. IN Some cultures, People DON'T WORK aFter tHe age OF Sixty-Five, aND Some Stop even earlier.

- APPRECIATE THAT WE ARE REALLY COOL, AND WE UP THE COOL LEVEL OF THE PARK BY BEING HERE.

# Park Policies

The park management would like to take this opportunity to remind employees of several policies that should be put into practice:

- The safety of park employees and visitors should be top of mind for all park workers.
- In case of extreme weather, please secure your job site and proceed to a safe location.

> DUDE, IN AN EMERGENCY? RUN LIKE THE WIND, MAN! RUN LIKE THE WIND!

> BUT WHAT IF THE WIND IS CAUSING THE PROBLEM, RIGBY? RUN WITH THE WIND, PERHAPS?

- Using the park phone for personal calls is strictly forbidden.
- All e-mails are the property of the Park.

> YOU CAN'T OWN E-MAILS!

> YEAH, E-MAILS BELONG TO THE INTERNET!

- **Do not post photos online of park employees without their consent.**

- **Park equipment is to be used for work purposes only.**

DON'T EVEN TRY TO TAKE OUR SWEET WHEELS AWAY FROM US.

*DO YOU MEAN YOUR GOLF CART, RIGBY? I SEE EYE TO EYE WITH YOU ON THAT — EVERY MAN NEEDS HIS OWN TRANSPORTATION VEHICLE!*

**The Park recognizes that many of our employees look forward to getting promoted.**

OF COURSE PEOPLE WANT TO GET PROMOTED. WHY ARE YOU PUTTING REALLY OBVIOUS THINGS IN HERE? WE ALREADY KNOW THIS STUFF!

THIS NEXT SECTION WAS SO STUPID THAT I JUST REWROTE IT. THIS IS THE REAL WAY YOU GET PROMOTED:

- **Not getting caught playing video games on work time**

- **Telling your boss he's always right.**

I AM ALWAYS RIGHT. I'M THE BOSS.

- **Pretend that listening to all of Benson's problems is an interesting thing to do.**

- **Have no life outside the Park.**

ISN'T IT TIME FOR SOME RULES ABOUT HOW WE CAN GET **OUT** OF FOLLOWING BENSON'S STUPID HANDBOOK AND SPEND OUR DAYS TRYING TO DO AS LITTLE AS POSSIBLE BY ANY MEANS NECESSARY? THAT'S A BOOK I'D WANT TO READ. I MIGHT EVEN PAY FOR IT INSTEAD OF DOWNLOADING IT ILLEGALLY.

RULES ARE IMPORTANT. WITHOUT RULES, SOCIETY WOULD FALL INTO CHAOS.

YES, DESPITE POPULAR OPINION AMONG CERTAIN SLACKERS, RULES AREN'T MADE TO BE BROKEN. THEY'RE MADE TO BE FOLLOWED. CLOSELY.

**EIGHT THINGS YOU WILL NEVER HEAR COMING OUT OF BENSON'S MOUTH:**

I TRUST YOU.

GREAT JOB!

TAKE THE AFTERNOON OFF—YOU
   DESERVE IT.

LOOKS LIKE SOMEONE IS HEADED
   TOWARD A PROMOTION.

DRINKS ARE ON ME, GUYS!

I'M PROUD OF YOU.

HERE'S YOUR BONUS CHECK.

I'M GLAD YOU WORK HERE.

RIGbY'S TOP FIVE SLACKER EXCUSES
NEVER FEAR, THE RIGSTER IS HERE,
giving YOU THE best JUSTIFICATIONS
FOR NOT getting THE JOb DONE:

1. THAT'S SO CRAZY, I WAS JUST
   abOUT to DO THAT.
2. YOU WANTED THAT DONE *NOW*?
3. WAIT A MINUTE . . . I THOUGHT
   SKIPS/MUSCLE MAN/POPS WAS
   DOING THAT!
4. YOU KNOW ME—ALWAYS A
   PERFECTIONIST. IF I CAN'T DO IT
   RIGHT, I JUST WON'T DO IT AT ALL.
5. I CAN'T DO EVERYTHING AROUND
   HERE, YOU KNOW.

## Releasing Employee Records and Information

Well, that's about all I have to say, people. Like I said, everything you need to know about working in the Park is here. I hope it helps you to do your best work, and appreciate your value in the Park family.

YOU'RE MY FAMILY, MORDECAI.

DUDE, YOU'RE MAKING ME UNCOMFORTABLE.

Yours truly,

Benson, Park Manager

PS: Keep up the good work!